# The Big Contest

Many, many years ago in t
were very bad and did man
make him unhappy and ang
a man called Ahab. God
obeyed him, one of these was a man called Elijah. Read
on and do the puzzles to find out what happened in the
contest between good and evil.

## Colour in the picture

One day Elijah gave King Ahab a message from God...

Starting at the letter A follow the letters from left to right and then from right to left until you come to the last letter.

**Start here** ⟶

| A | S | G | O | D | W | H | O | M | I | S | E |
|---|---|---|---|---|---|---|---|---|---|---|---|
| R | E | H | T | S | E | V | I | L | E | V | R |
| E | W | I | L | L | B | E | N | O | R | A | I |
| E | H | T | N | I | W | E | D | R | O | N | N |
| N | E | X | T | F | E | W | Y | E | A | R | S |
| O | S | Y | A | S | I | S | S | E | L | N | U |

Write out the message here

— —  — — —  — — — —  —  — — — — —  — — — — —

— — — — —  — — — —  — —  — —  — — — —  — — —

— — —  — —  — — —  — — —  — — — — —

— — — — — —  —  — — —  — —.

Which of these pictures does this verse say will happen?

God then gave Elijah another message.

Finish off this picture and then find the hidden letters. These will tell you where Elijah is going.

He was to leave the place where he was and go to the -

— — — — — —    — — — — —

and hide there.  (1 Kings 17:3)

Elijah did as he was told and went. He arrived at the place he was to hide and there was a brook there for him to drink from but ............ no food.

However God had a special way of getting food for his servant. Every morning and evening a special delivery came. It was made by

### V    E    R    A    N    S

— — — — — —

Unscramble the letters to find out who made the delivery.

Now draw these Ravens into the picture and make them carry the food. Unscramble these words to find out what food they are bringing to Elijah?

**t a e M**                    **d e a r B**

\_\_ \_\_ \_\_ \_\_                    \_\_ \_\_ \_\_ \_\_ \_\_

Finish colouring in the picture

After a time the brook dried up. Why do you think this happened? Look up 1 Kings 17:7.

_____

_____

What would happen to Elijah now?
As always God was there looking after him.
Use the pictures to finish the story.

God told __ __ __ __ __ __ to go to Zarephath.

He came to the __ __ __ __ gate

and met a widow gathering __ __ __ __ __ __ .

Elijah called to her and asked for some __ __ __ __ __ __

and a piece of __ __ __ __ __ .

She replied " I don't have any __ __ __ __ __ __

only a little __ __ __ __ __ __ and

some oil in a __ __ __ .

I am going to gather some __ __ __ __ __ __ __

to take __ __ __ __

and make us a last __ __ __ __

for myself and my son.

Then we will die."

Elijah told her to go home and do as she had planned but first make a little cake of bread for him and bring it to him. God said that her oil and flour would not run out until the rains came. Did she do as she was told?

5

Follow the packets of flour, drops of oil and loaves of bread to find out if the widow did as she was told.

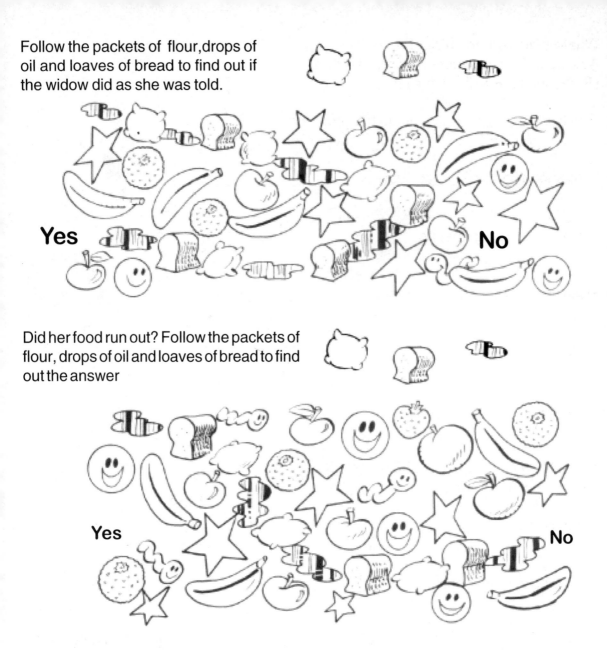

**Yes**

**No**

Did her food run out? Follow the packets of flour, drops of oil and loaves of bread to find out the answer

**Yes**

**No**

Sadly not long after all this happened the woman's son became ill, so ill in fact that he actually stopped breathing. The woman felt that things were unfair and asked Elijah if he had planned for her son to die.

Now Elijah had a room at the very top of the house and he took the boy from the woman and carried him up there. He laid him on the bed and called to God to bring life back to the boy. He called three times to God and then the boy began to breathe again. Elijah carried him back to his mother.

Cross out all the times the letters b and q appear in the sentence and you will find out what the widow said to Elijah.

Nobbqw I qkbnqoqbbw btqhaqbt ybqoqu aqqbbre a mqbaqbnq qobf Gqobd aqbndb bwbqhqaqt qyobqu    sqbaqy iqs btqrqube.

Write it out here.  ___ _ _____ ____ ___ ____ _

___ __ ___ ____ ____ ___ ___ __ ____

Ahab was the king of Israel at this time and there was still no rain in the land. God gave Elijah another message. Find out what it was by following the clouds in the puzzle below. These read from left to right. Then find out where it is in the Bible by following the sun pictures.

Help Elijah find his way to King Ahab.

There was another important man who was in charge of the king's palace. Find the letters of his name inside the picture.

___ ___ ___ ___ ___ ___ ___ ___

**FACT** - Elijah wore clothes made of hair and a leather belt.

**FACT** - Jezebel is Ahab's wife

**FACT** - When the Lord's prophets were being killed by King Ahab's wife, Queen Jezebel, Obadiah took some of the prophets and hid them in two caves. He kept them going with food and water.

Ahab had searched everywhere for Elijah because he was one of God's people. Ahab would have killed him too. But Ahab had not found him. King Ahab's secret police have forgotten to fill in this Wanted poster for Elijah. Can you work out which words go where?

Name _ _ _ _ _ _          Occupation _ _ _ _ _ _ _

Wears _ _ _ _ _ clothes and a _ _ _ _ _ _ _ belt.

He is one of _ _ _'s _ _ _ _ _ _ _ and an enemy of King

_ _ _ _ and his wife _ _ _ _ _ _ _ because they don't

like him as he keeps telling them to _ _ _ _ God.

(Answers: hairy, Prophet, people, Ahab, leather, Jezebel, obey, Elijah, God)

The drought was so bad that there was no grass for the horses and mules to eat and it was looking as if they would need to kill some of them. So, King Ahab set out with Obadiah to search for food. Ahab went one way and Obadiah went the other way.

When there is a drought people are short of water. What sort of things would you not be able to do in a drought? Unjumble the following words to find out three things you can't do without water...

**wism** __ __ __ __          **rindk** __ __ __ __ __          **wsha** __ __ __ __

How many things are there in this picture that you would need water for? How many cats can you spot hiding in the picture and how many mice?

As Obadiah went on his way, he met Elijah. Elijah told him to go and tell King Ahab that Elijah was there. Obadiah was afraid that Ahab would kill him or Elijah or both of them. They did however meet and King Ahab demanded to know what Elijah wanted.

King Ahab thought Elijah had brought trouble on the land but Elijah reminded him that he was the one who had caused trouble because... Crack the code to find out.

| a | b | c | d | e | f | g | h | i | j | k | l |
|---|---|---|---|---|---|---|---|---|---|---|---|
| 1 | 2 | 3 | 4 | 5 | 6 | 7 | 8 | 9 | 10 | 11 | 12 |
| m | n | o | p | q | r | s | t | u | v | w | x |
| 13 | 14 | 15 | 16 | 17 | 18 | 19 | 20 | 21 | 22 | 23 | 24 |

| y | z |
|---|---|
| 25 | 26 |

8.5     8.1.4     1.2.1.14.4.15.14.5.4     7.15.4.19

__ __    __ __ __    __ __ __ __ __ __ __ __ __ __ __    __ __ __ __

3.15.13.13.1.14.4.19.     1.14.4.     6.15.12.12.15.23.5.4.

__ __ __ __ __ __ __ __ __    __ __ __    __ __ __ __ __ __ __ __

2.1.1.12.

__ __ __ __

11

A meeting was arranged for Elijah, the people of Israel and the prophets of Baal. They were to meet on mount Carmel.

The people were to decide who is God. Was it the Lord God (Elijah's God) or was it Baal?

The people said nothing.

Elijah made a challenge.

Unscramble the sentences to see what it was.

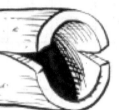

1  two bulls
   Get us
   for.

2  choose one
   Let prophets
   the

3  it Cut wood
   up put on it
   and

4  Elijah the
   same do
   would

5  call on their
   would god
   Each.

6  The fire who god
   answers is by
   God true the

From morning until night the prophets called on their god. Elijah taunted them and they shouted louder. They danced and they even cut themselves but no fire came.

Now it was Elijahs turn to try.  The scene was set as before but this time Elijah asked for something else to be added.  Can you find out from the picture what it was.

What things did Elijah ask to be added and how many are there?  Elijah told the people to fill them with water and to pour the water over the fire, three times in all. How many jar full's of water would that be? Write out the sum below and work out the answer.

_____ X _____ = _____

Work It Out

Next Elijah prayed to his God. The fire of the Lord fell on the sacrifice and everything was all burned up. What happened next? Tick the answers you think are correct.

The fire burned everything up and the people ran away.

or

The people worshipped God.

A party was held to honour the prophets.

or

The prophets of Baal were seized and then killed.

Rica came.

Rain came.

or

The drought continued.

The king went to eat and drink but Elijah went off to the top of a mountain where he prayed. He had a servant with him and he was sent to look out for a cloud that would show the rain really was coming. Elijah sent him to look towards the sea but there was no sign of rain.

Eventually on the seventh time there could be seen a tiny cloud. The servant was sent to tell King Ahab to hitch up his chariot and go home to Jezreel before the rain stopped him. Then the sky grew black with clouds, the wind rose and a heavy rain came down. The power of the Lord came on Elijah and he managed to run ahead of King Ahab and his chariot.

Draw Elijah into the picture running ahead of the chariot. As well as Elijah there are three things missing in this picture. What are they? Draw them into the picture before colouring it in.

Can you find all these words in the wordsearch?

Elijah, Baal, Ahab, Jezreel, Jezebel, Kerith, Ravine, Zarephath, Ravens, Prophets, Widow, Oil, Drink, Bread, Bull, Sacrifice, Flour, Obadiah, Chariot, Drought, Water

| O | B | A | D | I | A | H | L | M | R | E | T | A | W |
|---|---|---|---|---|---|---|---|---|---|---|---|---|---|
| I | C | D | P | R | O | P | H | E | T | S | X | D | I |
| L | B | B | A | A | L | H | B | N | K | N | I | R | D |
| U | R | B | P | V | K | E | R | I | T | H | W | O | O |
| Z | J | T | W | E | V | A | D | U | T | K | Q | U | W |
| T | R | E | M | N | D | T | G | A | O | F | L | G | C |
| O | A | L | Z | S | F | L | H | H | P | L | T | H | E |
| I | V | I | G | R | P | P | K | A | U | O | F | T | S |
| R | I | J | S | E | E | Q | R | B | R | E | A | D | L |
| A | N | A | R | R | H | E | Y | N | I | J | Y | U | A |
| H | E | H | A | Z | C | O | L | E | B | E | Z | E | J |
| C | V | Z | S | A | C | R | I | F | I | C | E | V | S |

Now when King Ahab met Jezebel he told her all that had happened and how the prophets of Baal had been killed because of Elijah. In return Jezebel sent a message to Elijah, warning him that she would have the same done to him by the next day.

Elijah was terrified.

What other words might describe how he was feeling? What emotions can you find in this wordsearch? There are ten possible answers. Work out which of these emotions would fit Elijah at this time?

| S | G | R | E | A | T | J | A | G |
|---|---|---|---|---|---|---|---|---|
| B | C | O | N | D | L | O | N | O |
| R | H | A | P | P | Y | Y | X | O |
| S | T | B | R | L | S | F | I | D |
| S | A | D | B | E | M | U | O | K |
| B | A | D | P | Q | D | L | U | S |
| W | O | R | R | I | E | D | S | S |
| D | E | P | R | E | S | S | E | D |

Elijah ran away.  Find out where he went to first. The word in the sign is back to front. Try placing it up against a mirror to find out where Elijah is running to in such a hurry.

— — — — — — — — — — —

Elijah then travelled alone into the desert. He found a broom tree, sat down and prayed to God. He asked God to let him die. He lay down by the tree and slept. Then he had an amazing experience. An angel told him to get up and eat. What did he find by his head? Unjumble the following words and then circle the pictures that correspond to the answers.

**mose   rebda      dna   a   ajr   fo   tawre**

_ _ _ _   _ _ _ _ _      _ _ _   _   _ _ _   _ _   _ _ _ _ _

He got up and ate and drank and went back to sleep. The angel came again and the same thing happened. This time Elijah was warned that he had a long journey ahead. He travelled for a long time until he came to a place called Horeb, where he spent the night in a cave. To find out how many days Elijah travelled for count how many Cacti are growing outside the cave and then count how many wriggly worms you can find. Multiply the number of worms by the number of cacti.

What number did you get? _____

# CROSSWORD

**Across**

1. Elijah poured _ _ _ _ jars of water over the Sacrifice, three times.
3. What fed Elijah, can fly and squawks?
5. Elijah's story is in the book of _ _ _ _ _.
7. What was the occupation of Jezebel?
11. God is the _ _ _ true God.
12. What did the angel leave Elijah to drink?
14. How did Elijah get to Jezreel? He _ _ _.
15. How many times were the jars of water poured over the sacrifice?
16. What was Elijah's occupation?

**Down**

1 How many days did Elijah travel to get to Horeb?
2 For three years the land of Israel was dry because there was no _ _ _ _.
4 Jesus Christ died to save us from our _ _ _ _.
5 What was the occupation of Ahab?
6 What was the occupation of Obadiah?
8 What was the sacrifice placed on?
9 Who is the only one we should worship?
10 What did the angel give Elijah to eat?
12 Jezebel was King Ahab's _ _ _ _.
13 Elijah's sacrifice was all _ _ _ _ _ up.

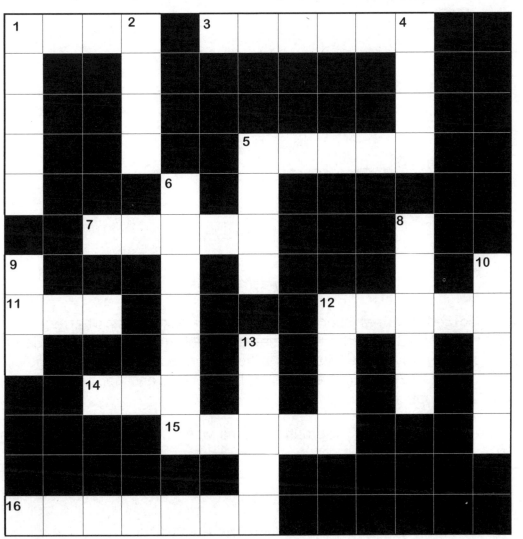

Elijah was probably very scared while he was in the cave because he thought he was the only prophet left and now it looked as if he might be killed too. Now God spoke to him and told him to leave the cave and go out onto the mountain because the Lord was about to pass by there.

Three tremendous things happened out on the mountain. What were they? Unjumble the letters to find out.

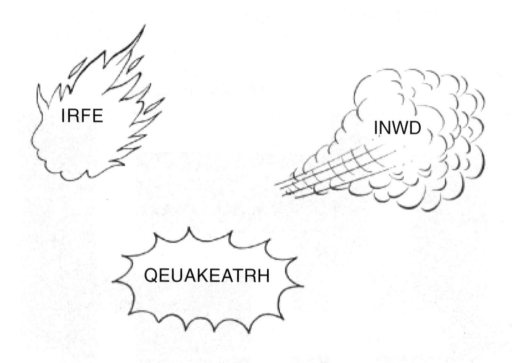

IRFE

INWD

QEUAKEATRH

But the Lord wasn't in these.

When they had died down a whisper came and the voice asked Elijah what he was doing there. Elijah again told God how he felt and how he thought he was going to be killed. God wasn't in any of the noisy, tremendous things that happened but he was in the quiet little whisper. God then told Elijah to go back the way he had come and then to anoint two new kings and also a prophet to succeed him .

The prophet's name was

# ELISHA

He was very busy when Elijah found him.

What do you think he was doing? 1 Kings 19:19

eating his breakfast

going on a hike

riding his donkey

playing football

fixing a car

Watching a television

ploughing with oxen

mowing the lawn

Elijah threw his coat around Elisha which was a sign that Elisha was to take over Elijah's job when he was no longer there to do it. Elisha left his work and all he had and went and followed Elijah and became his helper. These two spent time together and Elisha learned from Elijah.

Eventually it was time for Elijah to leave Elisha and this happened in an amazing way .

Elijah tried to get Elisha to leave him on his own but wherever Elijah went Elisha went too because he knew that soon they would be parted. Eventually they came to the river Jordan and needed to get across.

How could they get across?
Unjumble the words - the pictures will
give you an extra clue.

Did Elijah and Elisha

- lais ni a toab?

— — — —   — —   —   — — —

Did Elijah and Elisha

- duilb a ridbge?

— — — — —   —   — — — —

Did Elijah and Elisha

- mujp rossac?

— — — —   — — — — — —

Did Elijah and Elisha

- wism?

— — — —

No. Elijah took his cloak, rolled it up and touched the water with it, a path was made in the middle and they crossed over. (2 Kings 2:8) Draw what happened in this space below.

Suddenly a chariot of fire appeared and Elijah was caught up to heaven. Elisha ran and picked up the cloak that had fallen . He took it to the Jordan and used it as Elijah had and the same thing happened, the water split.

Colour in the picture of Elijah in the firey chariot.

This was a sign that God was with Elisha now and he could carry on the work that Elijah had been doing. Work out what the other prophets did when Elisha returned. Cross out all the z's and q's to find out what happened next.

Tzhqe  pzzrqzophqqeztsz  sqzeqznqt  fzzifqtqy  mzqezn,  wqqhzo

szzeqazqrqzchzqed  fqqozr  tzzhqreze  dqqazyzs  bqquzt  dzzqid

nqzqozt  fzziqnqd  Ezzliqqjazh.  Wzzhen  tzzheqy  rzzetqqurzneqd

tzzqo  Ezzqliszzqha  hzze  sqqaiqqd  tqqo  tzzheqm,  'Dzqidqqn't

I  tqqezll  yzoqu  nzoqt  tzzo  gqzo.'

_ _ _   _ _ _ _ _ _ _ _   _ _ _ _   _ _ _ _ _   _ _ _ , _ _ _

_ _ _ _ _ _ _   _ _ _   _ _ _ _   _ _ _ _   _ _ _   _ _ _   _ _ _   _ _ _ _

_ _ _ _ _ _ .   _ _ _ _   _ _ _   _ _ _ _ _   _ _   _ _ _ _ _ _   _ _   _ _ _ _

_ _   _ _ _ _   " _ _ _ _ _   _   _ _ _ _   _ _ _   _ _ _   _ _   _ _ . "

Elijah and Elisha followed God. Elisha carried on the work of God that Elijah had started. On this page there is a Bible verse puzzle to work out. Start where the arrow is pointing at and read round.

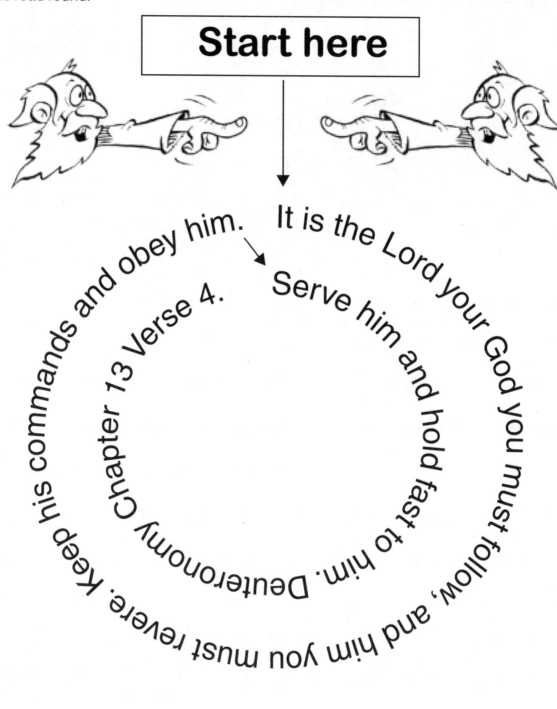

**Start here**

It is the Lord your God you must follow, and him you must revere. Keep his commands and obey him. Serve him and hold fast to him. Deuteronomy Chapter 13 Verse 4.

# Wiggley Worms

Some worms have been running around on this page and have gotten all the Bible verses mixed up. See if you can help unwiggle them.

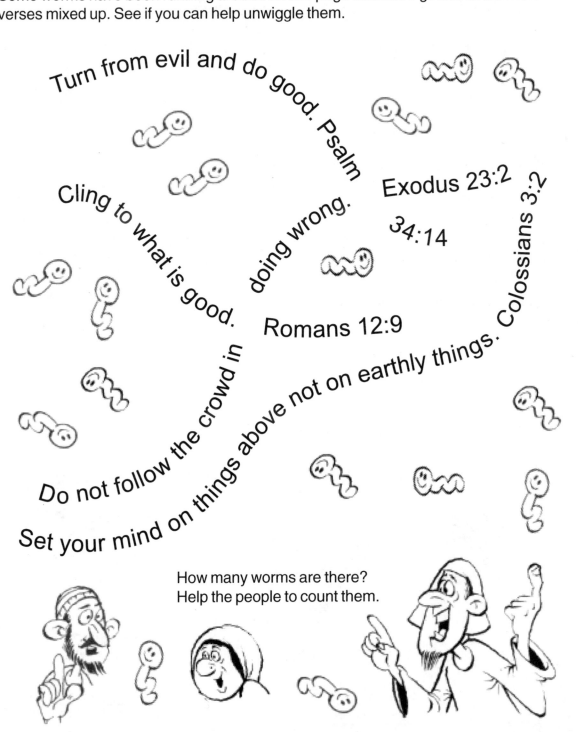

Turn from evil and do good. Psalm

Cling to what is good.

doing wrong.

Exodus 23:2

34:14

Colossians 3:2

Romans 12:9

Do not follow the crowd in

Set your mind on things above not on earthly things.

How many worms are there?
Help the people to count them.

# How well do you remember?

Fill in the blank spaces or circle the right answer.

1. What was Elijahs job? - prophet  priest  king

2. Who was the King?  Ahab     Aaron    Adam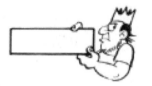

3. Who was the kings wife?

Jessica    Jezreel    Jezebel

4. Which of these birds brought food to Elijah?

vultures

ravens

robins

5. What are you short of in a drought?

wind

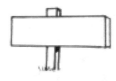

sun

rain

6. Who did Elijah help when they were ill?

Elisha, Ahab or a boy

7. At the contest, what did Elijah ask for?

 sheep

 horses

 bulls

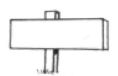

8. Who was in charge of the kings palace?

Obed

Obadaiah

Eli

9. What were Elijahs clothes made from?
Remember he wore a belt as well.

silk and cotton, wool and linen, or hair and  leather

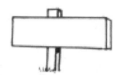

10.  How many times was water poured on the fire?

5        3        7

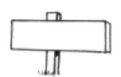

11.  Who took over from Elijah?

Ahab

Elisha

Enoch

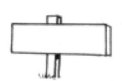

28

In that puzzle there were eleven questions to answer.
For every answer you get correct colour in a jar of water.
Once you are finished the puzzle
you can colour in the rest of the picture.

# ANSWERS

p2      As God whom I serve lives there will be no rain nor dew in the next few years unless I say so.
Picture 1.

p3.      Kerith Ravine

p4.      Ravens; meat; bread; There was a drought on.

p5      Elijah, town, sticks, water, bread, bread, flour, jug, sticks, home, meal.

p5/6      Yes; No

p7      Now I know that you are a man of God and what you say is true
Go and present yourself to the king and then I will send rain. 1 Kings 18 Verse 1

p8      Route B; Obadiah

p9      Elijah; Prophet; hairy; leather; God's; people; Ahab; Jezebel; obey.

p10      Swim; drink; wash
Picture: You need water for at least six things.
Washing the car; Watering the plants; Swimming; Fish pond; Washing clothes; having a drink.
Five mice; Two cats

p11      He had abandoned Gods commands and followed Baal.

p12      Get two bulls for us;      Let the prophets choose one;
Cut it up and put it on wood;      Elijah would do the same
Each would call on their God;      The God who answers by fire is the true God.

p13      Four jars of water
Four jars of water three times = 12 jars of water in total.

p14      The people worshipped God; The prophets were seized and killed; Rain came.

p15      Chariot wheels and the horses reins and the black rain clouds.

p16      Wordsearch solutions (see opposite page.)

p 17      Emotions: great; good, happy; joyful.
What Elijah would have felt: anxious; bad; sad; worried; depressed; scared
Beersheba

p18      Some bread; and a jar of water; 4 Cacti; 10 worms = 40 days.

p 19      Cross Word Solutions: **Across** 1. Four; 3. Ravens; 5. Kings; 7. Queen;
11. One; 12. Water; 14. ran; 15. Three; 16. Prophet.
**Down**: 1. Forty; 2. Rain; 4. Sins; 5. King; 6. Servant; 8. Altar; 9. God;
10. Bread; 12. Wife; 13. Burnt.

p20      Fire; Wind; Earthquake.

p21      ploughing with oxen

p22      Did Elijah and Elisha sail in a boat? build a bridge? jump across? Swim?

p23      The prophets sent fifty men, who searched for three days but did not find Elijah. When they returned to Elisha he said to them, 'Didn't I tell you not to go.'

p24      It is the Lord your God you must follow, and him you must revere. Keep his commands and obey him. Serve him and hold fast to him.
Deuteronomy Chapter 13 Verse 4.

| O | B | A | D | I | A | H | L | M | R | E | T | A | W |
|---|---|---|---|---|---|---|---|---|---|---|---|---|---|
| I | C | D | P | R | O | P | H | E | T | S | X | D | I |
| L | B | B | A | A | L | H | B | N | K | N | I | R | D |
| U | R | B | P | V | K | E | R | I | T | H | W | O | O |
| Z | J | T | W | E | V | A | D | U | T | K | Q | U | W |
| T | R | E | M | N | D | T | G | A | O | F | L | G | C |
| O | A | L | Z | S | F | L | H | H | P | L | T | H | E |
| I | V | I | G | R | P | P | K | A | U | O | F | T | S |
| R | I | J | S | E | E | Q | R | B | R | E | A | D | L |
| A | N | A | R | R | H | E | Y | N | I | J | Y | U | A |
| H | E | H | A | Z | C | O | L | E | B | E | Z | E | J |
| C | V | Z | S | A | C | R | I | F | I | C | E | V | S |

p25  Set your mind on things above not on earthly things. Colossians 3:2
   Do not follow the crowd in doing wrong. Exodus 23:2.
   Turn from evil and do good. Psalm 34:14.
   Cling to what is good. Romans 12:9.
   Sixteen worms.

p26-28 Prophet; Ahab; Jezebel; ravens;rain; A boy; bulls;Obadiah; hair and leather; three; Elisha.

Text by Ruth Maclean
Illustrations by Barrie Appleby

Printed in Great Britain by JW Arrowsmith
ISBN 1 85792 472 X
Published by Christian Focus Publications
Geanies House, Fearn, Tain, Ross-shire, IV20 1TW, Scotland
www.christianfocus.com

Do you like puzzles? Have you enjoyed this book? Here are further puzzles for you to enjoy...

**The beautiful bride - Rebecca**
ISBN 1 85792 1399

**The Brave Ruler - Daniel**
ISBN 1 85792 0880

**God's Builder - Nehemiah**
1 85792 0538

**The Great Celebration - Hezekiah**
ISBN 1 85792 1380

**The Happy Harvest - Ruth**
ISBN 1 85792 2468

**The Man who Ran - Jonah**
ISBN 1 85792 228X

**The Queen's Feast - Esther**
ISBN 1 85792 0899

**The Wise King - Solomon**
ISBN 1 85792 052X

**The Shepherd King - David**
ISBN 1 85792 3030

**The Desert Leader - Moses**
ISBN 1 85792 3049

**Journey to Jericho - Joshua**
ISBN 1 85792 4738

Published by Christian Focus Publications
Geanies House, Fearn, Tain, Ross-shire, IV20 1TW, Scotland
**www.christianfocus.com**